2009
STAKEHOLDER REPORT

DEFENSE SECURITY SERVICE

MESSAGE FROM DSS DIRECTOR

I am pleased to present the first Stakeholder Report of the Defense Security Service (DSS). When I meet with Congressional staffers or acquisition personnel in the Department of Defense (DoD), I'm often asked, "What is the clearance backlog?" Since DoD transferred the personnel security investigation mission to the Office of Personnel Management in 2005, it is clear to me that DSS needs to do a much better job at keeping all of you — our agency stakeholders — better informed of what is happening at DSS and where we are going.

DSS underwent a major transformation over the past two years. DSS is now streamlined and has reorganized and refocused on two core missions — oversight of the National Industrial Security Program (NISP) and delivering Security Education to the government and industry security communities. We are making great strides in this regard. In these pages, you will learn about our most recent successes and our focus for the future. We've also presented case studies that show how DSS is refining its processes to be more operationally agile and flexible in responding to requirements. In the final case study, there are a number of lessons learned that we will apply across the agency to ensure we are doing everything possible to identify and mitigate the insider threat.

The NISP is the cornerstone in the Department of Defense to protect our leading edge research and technology from compromise. DSS takes its community responsibility as the NISP Executive Agent seriously. We understand that globalization and the active efforts of our friends and adversaries to acquire restricted technologies have not abated. The challenges for DSS have increased accordingly. I am committed to the continued transformation of DSS from the troubled agency of the recent past, to a more robust, healthy organization that it is quickly becoming.

Thank you for reading and I look forward to sharing more of the changes at DSS with you in future Stakeholder Reports.

Kathleen M. Watson
Director

VISION:

DSS is the premier provider of personnel and industrial security services in the Department of Defense (DoD), improving the security of our nation and its warfighters.

> **THE BASIC NATURE OF MAN AND THE IRON REALITIES OF NATIONS HAVE NOT CHANGED. WHAT HAS CHANGED IS THAT THE INTERNATIONAL ENVIRONMENT TODAY IS MORE COMPLEX, AND MORE DANGEROUS, THAN IT HAS BEEN IN MANY DECADES.**
>
> **SECDEF ROBERT M. GATES**

MISSION:

DSS supports national security and the warfighter, secures the nation's technological base, and oversees the protection of U.S. and foreign classified information in the hands of industry.

We accomplish this mission by: Clearing industrial facilities, personnel and associated information systems; collecting, analyzing and referring threat information to industry and government partners; managing foreign ownership, control, or influence in cleared industry; providing advice and oversight to industry; delivering security education and training; and, providing information technology services that support the industrial security mission of DoD and its partner agencies.

STRATEGIC GOALS:

To Think and Act Strategically
To Earn and Maintain Stakeholder Support
To Achieve Operational Excellence
To Consistently Satisfy our Customers

> **INFORMATION IS OUR GREATEST STRATEGIC ASSET.**
>
> **HONORABLE JOHN GRIMES,**
> **ASD(NII) / DoD CIO**

HISTORY:

Establishment of the Defense Security Service

The Defense Security Service (DSS), formerly known as the Defense Investigative Service (DIS) was established on Jan. 1, 1972. DSS was created in response to President Richard M. Nixon's approval of proposals suggesting the reorganization of the national intelligence community and the creation of an "Office of Defense Investigation" to consolidate Department of Defense (DoD) personnel security investigations (PSI). Prior to this consolidation, such work was accomplished through U.S. military departments by four major DoD investigative agencies. They were: 1) the U.S. Army Intelligence Command, 2) the U.S. Army Criminal Investigative Command, 3) the Naval Investigative Service, and 4) the Office of Special Investigations, Air Force.

The Early Years

DSS was an organization whose manpower, facilities and operational structure were almost entirely borrowed from the Army, Navy and Air Force and the initial months of the agency's existence proved turbulent. As DSS matured, military personnel gradually returned to their parent services and the workforce became entirely civilian. Additional security functions were transferred to DSS, to include the transfer of administration of the Defense Industrial Security Program from the Defense Logistics Agency (DLA) to DSS on Oct. 2, 1980.

The Year of the Spy

In 1985, Secretary of Defense, Caspar Weinberger, established the Stilwell Commission in response to the alarming increase of espionage cases against the U.S. government. The Stilwell Commission was directed to review and evaluate security policies and procedures in DoD. The Commission's recommendations directly impacted DSS, as they believed increased priority should be given to DoD security efforts and that necessary resourcing must be made available. As a result, Congress increased DSS funding by $25 million in fiscal year 1986, with an emphasis on Periodic Reinvestigations.

Significant Enhancements during the Last Decade

In May 1993, DSS established a counterintelligence (CI) office in response to the dramatic changes taking place in the defense marketplace and the growing need for current and relevant intelligence-threat data by the DSS workforce and industrial managers.

The personnel security investigation (PSI) mission transferred from the DoD to the Office of Personnel Management (OPM) effective Feb. 20, 2005. DSS retained the function, on behalf of DoD, to oversee the OPM billing and financial reconciliation process for PSIs for the entire Department. Additionally, DSS retained the adjudication of personnel security clearances for industry, the projection of industry personnel security clearance requirements, and funding of industry clearance investigations.

On Jan. 15, 2009, the Deputy Secretary of Defense signed a memorandum directing DSS to move forward on enhancing the National Industrial Security Program and reinvigorating the Security Education Training and Awareness Program, in an effort to "strengthen and refocus DSS to meet 21st century industrial security and counterintelligence needs."

> **THE DEPARTMENT OF DEFENSE WILL HAVE TO PLAN FOR A FUTURE SECURITY ENVIRONMENT SHAPED BY THE INTERACTION OF POWERFUL STRATEGIC TRENDS. THESE TRENDS SUGGEST A RANGE OF PLAUSIBLE FUTURES, SOME PRESENTING MAJOR CHALLENGES AND SECURITY RISKS.**
>
> **2008 NATIONAL DEFENSE STRATEGY**

DSS Seal

The three divisions of the shield refer to the three basic requirements of all investigations: patient inquiry, observation, and careful examination of the facts.

The eagle, adopted from that used in the seal of DoD, alludes to keenness of vision, strength, and tenacity that symbolizes DSS.

The three arrows, also adopted from the seal of DoD, refer to the Armed Services, comprising the military components of DSS. In crossing over and protectively covering the Pentagon, these arrows represent the DoD wide aspects of the DSS mission.

The color dark blue, the National color, represents the United States, and the color light blue represents DoD, the shade of blue being used by the Defense Department. The pattern indicates the integral unity of the U.S., DoD, and DSS. The color gold (or yellow) is symbolic of zeal and achievement.

On a white disc within a border of blue with gold outer rim is the shield of DSS in full color blazoned above a wreath of laurel and olive proper (as depicted on the DoD seal). Inscribed at top of the white disc is "Defense Security Service" and in the base, in smaller letters, is "United States of America," all letters gold.

The laurel and olives symbolize merit and peace; the color white signifies "deeds worthy of remembrance."

THE NATIONAL SECURITY AND ECONOMIC HEALTH OF THE UNITED STATES DEPEND ON THE SECURITY, STABILITY, AND INTEGRITY OF OUR NATION'S CYBERSPACE, BOTH IN THE PUBLIC AND PRIVATE SECTORS. THE PRESIDENT IS CONFIDENT THAT WE CAN PROTECT OUR NATION'S CRITICAL CYBER INFRASTRUCTURE WHILE AT THE SAME TIME ADHERING TO THE RULE OF LAW AND SAFEGUARDING PRIVACY RIGHTS AND CIVIL LIBERTIES.

ASSISTANT TO THE PRESIDENT FOR COUNTERTERRORISM AND HOMELAND SECURITY JOHN BRENNAN

> **OUR TRANSFORMATION TO A 21ST CENTURY, NET CENTRIC FORCE IS, THEREFORE, DEPENDENT UPON ULTIMATE DELIVERY OF THE CRITICAL ENABLING CAPABILITIES THAT WILL:**
>
> **ALLOW INFORMATION TO BE ACCESSED AND SHARED, ENSURE PARTNERS CAN COLLABORATE, AND SUPPORT DECISION MAKERS AT ALL LEVELS TO MAKE BETTER DECISIONS FASTER AND TO TAKE ACTION SOONER.**
>
> HONORABLE JOHN GRIMES, ASD(NII) / DoD CIO

ORGANIZATIONAL OVERVIEW:

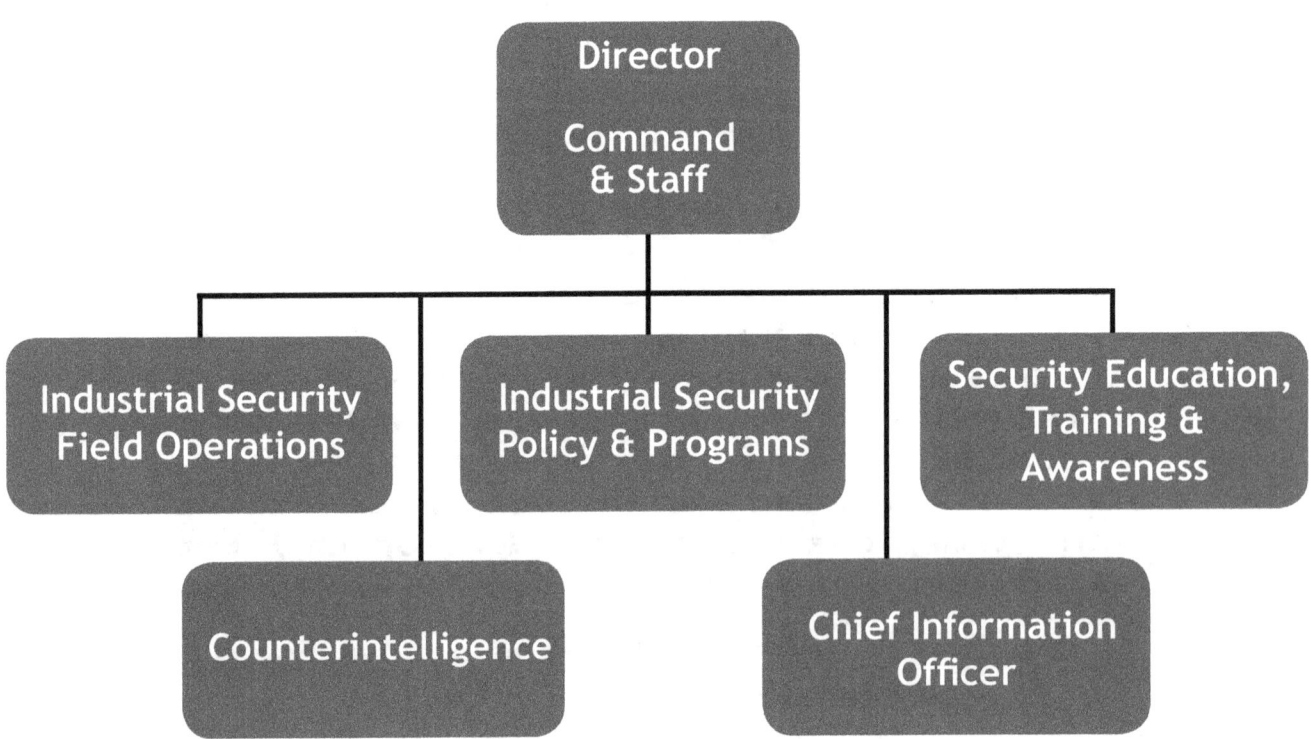

DSS Headquarters is located in Northern Virginia, with offices across the country

Capital Region, Arlington, VA	Northern Region, Boston, MA	Southern Region, Irving, TX	Western Region, San Diego, CA
Ft. Meade, MD	Groton, CT	Huntsville, AL	Anchorage, AK
Linthicum, MD	New Haven, CT	Homestead, FL	Phoenix, AZ
Arlington, VA	Boston, MA	Hurlburt Field, FL	Tucson, AZ
Chantilly, VA	Devens, MA	Orlando, FL	Camarillo, CA
Quantico, VA	Wilmington, MA	Patrick Air Force Base, FL	Dublin, CA
	Livonia, MI	Tampa, FL	Encino, CA
	Minneapolis-Fort Snelling, MN	Smyrna, GA	Huntington Beach, CA
	Mt. Laurel, NJ	Des Plaines, IL	March Air Force Base, CA
	Picatinny Arsenal, NJ	Indianapolis, IN	Palmdale, CA
	Buffalo, NY	Kansas City, KS	Pasadena, CA
	Syracuse-Liverpool, NY	St. Louis, MO	San Diego, CA
	Watervliet, NY	Charlotte, NC	Santa Barbara, CA
	Westbury, NY	Offutt Air Force Base, NE	Sunnyvale, CA
	Cincinnati, OH	Oklahoma City, OK	Travis Air Force Base, CA
	Cleveland, OH	Charleston, SC	Colorado Springs, CO
	Columbus, OH	San Antonio, TX	Denver, CO
	Wright-Patterson AFB, OH	Houston, TX	Honolulu, HI
	Annville, PA	Irving, TX	Albuquerque, NM
	Boyers, PA	Hampton, VA	El Paso, TX
	Philadelphia, PA	Virginia Beach, VA	Seattle, WA
	Pittsburgh, PA		
	Milwaukee, WI		

INDUSTRIAL SECURITY FIELD OPERATIONS:

Industrial Security Field Operations (ISFO) works with cleared industry on a daily basis to protect U.S. and foreign classified information

350 Industrial Security Representatives spread across the United States

- Provide advice and assistance
- Inspect facilities for compliance with established guidelines
- Report security incidents and provide remediation

Information System Security Professionals (ISSP)

- Provide technical expertise to identify key threats facing industry today
- Certify and accredit industry information systems

Defense Industrial Security Clearance Office adjudicates clearances for industry personnel

ISFO Facts:

12,647 active, cleared facilities in NISP

- 9,100 facility security inspections (FY08)
- 1,791 new facility clearances granted (FY08)
- 14,000 accredited systems in industry
- Average time for system accreditation: 33 days

Adjudicate Industry Security Clearances (DISCO)

- 1,278,299 cleared personnel
- 180,651 Personnel Security Adjudications (FY08)
- 16 days to adjudicate all initial clearances by IRTPA* measures

*Intelligence Reform and Terrorism Prevention Act of 2004 mandated specific goals for improving timelines for both personnel security investigations and adjudications.

> " INTELLIGENCE AND INFORMATION SHARING HAVE ALWAYS BEEN A VITAL COMPONENT OF NATIONAL SECURITY. RELIABLE INFORMATION AND ANALYSIS, QUICKLY AVAILABLE, IS AN ENDURING CHALLENGE. "
>
> 2008 NATIONAL DEFENSE STRATEGY

COUNTERINTELLIGENCE:

The DSS Counterintelligence (CI) Office works in concert with ISFO to identify threats to cleared industry

CI Specialists collect suspicious contact reports (SCRs) from industry
- Conduct an initial analysis
- Refer cases to the appropriate investigative agency for follow-up
- Use these SCRs to educate industry
- Provide information to the Intelligence Community

Focused on key threats to industry
- Cyber
- Insider threat
- Hard target nations

Supports all DSS operations
- Threat assessments for Foreign Ownership Control or Influence (FOCI) mitigation process
- Integrated into training courses at DSS Academy

CI Facts:

- 5,017 CI Suspicious Contact Reports (SCRs) (FY08)

- 1,403 CI Investigations or operational activities by other Government Agencies based on DSS SCR referrals

- 23 DSS referrals resulted in investigations by FBI, ICE, DCIS, NCIS, or Army

- 431 Personnel security clearances that were denied access eligibility based on input from DSS CI

- 124 SCRs with suspected foreign cyber attacks directed against unclassified systems within the Defense Industrial Base

- 389 Intelligence Information Reports

- 2,012 adjudicative files referred with legitimate CI or security concerns

- 17,207 cleared industry personnel received Counterintelligence Threat Awareness Briefings

> **THE GLOBALIZATION OF TECHNOLOGY IS NO LONGER A CHOICE FOR GOVERNMENTS PLANNING TO MODERNIZE THEIR MILITARY FORCES; IT IS A CHARACTERISTIC OF THE ENVIRONMENT IN WHICH MILITARY CAPABILITIES WILL BE DEVELOPED AND PRODUCED FOR THE FORESEEABLE FUTURE.**
>
> **WILLIAM SCHNEIDER, JR.,**
> **CHAIRMAN OF THE DEFENSE SCIENCE BOARD**

INDUSTRIAL SECURITY POLICY AND PROGRAMS

Industrial Security Policy and Programs office (ISPP) supports ISFO with

- Adjudication of foreign ownership, control or influence (FOCI)
- Implementation of FOCI countermeasures
- Administration of international programs
- Industrial and personnel security policy
- Projections for industry personnel security investigations
- Support SAP oversight at industrial facilities
- Analytic support

ISPP Facts:

- 643 FOCI facilities
- 240 FOCI mitigation agreements
- Support to 65 Foreign Countries
- NISP Support to 23 Government Agencies

> " INFORMATION IS A STRATEGIC ASSET. IT MUST BE GIVEN THE SAME PRIORITY AND PROTECTION AS ANY MISSION CRITICAL SYSTEM OR PLATFORM. SUCCESS IN DAY-TO-DAY PEACETIME FUNCTIONS, DURING STABILITY AND SUPPORT OPERATIONS, AND ARMED CONFLICT WILL BE DEPENDENT UPON OUR ABILITY TO CONNECT PEOPLE WITH INFORMATION AND CREATE AN INFORMATION ADVANTAGE FOR OUR TEAM AND OUR MISSION PARTNERS. "
>
> HONORABLE JOHN GRIMES, ASD(NII) / DoD CIO

SECURITY EDUCATION TRAINING AND AWARENESS

SETA delivers security education and training to DoD and the cleared contractor community through formal classroom, web-based and correspondence/distance learning

Security education includes core security disciplines
- ◦ Personnel
- ◦ Physical
- ◦ Industrial
- ◦ Special Access Programs

Accreditation for security professionals
- ◦ Special Access Programs
- ◦ Adjudicators
- ◦ DSS workforce
- ◦ Facility Security Officers

Integrate counterintelligence and information systems security into all courses

SETA Facts:

- 35,419 students trained to date (FY09)
- 53,569 students trained (FY08)
- 362% increase over FY04
- Deployed 10 new courses FY08/09
- 28 courses currently under development in conjunction with stakeholders or at request
- Deployed 8 new security information/job aid videos
- Developing 11 additional security information/job aid videos
- Fielded web accessible Resource Tool for Security Professionals

" THE ASD NII/DoD CIO PROVIDES THE LEADERSHIP THAT IS TURNING THE VISION, DELIVER THE POWER OF INFORMATION, INTO REALITY. "

HONORABLE JOHN GRIMES, ASD(NII) / DoD CIO

CHIEF INFORMATION OFFICER

The Office of Chief Information Officer (CIO) provides information technology services to DSS employees in 75 locations

- Classified and unclassified network connectivity
- Office automation and web services
- Computer security
- Information assurance/computer network defense

The CIO manages and maintains IT systems that support the industrial security and personnel security missions

- Joint Personnel Adjudication System (JPAS)*
- Industrial Security Facilities Database (ISFD)
- Defense Central Index of Investigations (DCII)*
- ENROL

*Scheduled to transition to Defense Manpower Data Center (DMDC)

CIO Facts:

- 100,000+ worldwide users
- 6 Legacy Security Systems
- 5 System Enhancements in Development

> " I WILL NEVER ABANDON - AND I WILL VIGOROUSLY DEFEND - THE NECESSITY OF CLASSIFICATION TO DEFEND OUR TROOPS AT WAR; TO PROTECT SOURCES AND METHODS; AND TO SAFEGUARD CONFIDENTIAL ACTIONS THAT KEEP THE AMERICAN PEOPLE SAFE. "
>
> **PRESIDENT BARACK OBAMA**

ACHIEVEMENTS
& CASE STUDIES

DSS continually assesses its oversight of the industrial security program to ensure the most robust mechanisms for the protection of classified information in industry are in place. During the past year DSS can cite many successes.

Better oversight of cleared industry
Facilities of Interest

Once a company is cleared, DSS has oversight authority to evaluate the security operations of the organization for compliance with the National Industrial Security Program. DSS developed a Facility of Interest List (FIL) in order to align resources towards a risk based inspection process.

The list determines the level of risk for over 12,000 facilities as they relate to the overall foreign threat specific to key technologies. This approach supports the National Counterintelligence Strategy of the United States as well as the DoD Counterintelligence Strategy.

The list established by DSS considered such factors as:

- Poor security ratings
- Invalidated facility clearances
- Foreign ownership
- Counterintelligence concerns
- Special Access Programs
- Arms, Ammunition and Explosives programs
- Critical Infrastructure Programs
- Critical National Assets
- Critical Program Information
- Trusted Foundries

The latest FIL was published on April 2, 2009 and identified 1,000 facilities.

DSS will continue to refine the risk factors to better incorporate assessments of counterintelligence threats to the cleared U.S. Defense Industry. The goal is a coordinated, integrated visit from DSS to the right facility, at the right time with appropriate resources resulting in a more effective, meaningful inspection.

Coordinated Inspection Process

DSS adopted a team approach to its oversight and inspection of cleared facilities. Day-to-day tactical control of Industrial Security Representative (IS Reps), field Counterintelligence Specialists and Information System Security Personnel (ISSPs) now rests with the local Field Office Chief and one of four Regional Directors. The result is a team-based approach to facility oversight by the personnel most familiar with the facilities and its challenges. Each high-risk facility will be assigned a team of experts who will work together to provide integrated oversight and support. During 2008, 193 of the 240 team inspections conducted by DSS were at FIL facilities.

DSS deployed FOCI and International Specialists to the field to provide increased expertise at the local level in these complex areas. These specialists work the front-end FOCI process by putting together less complex mitigation agreements and are fully integrated members of the field team. Their knowledge and insights result in better mitigation arrangements and oversight of companies under FOCI.

Counterintelligence
Refocused Priorities

The Counterintelligence (CI) team has aligned its focus to counter those dangers that pose the greatest threat to our nation's most critical assets:
- Hard Target Nations
- Insider Threats
- Cyber Threats
- Internal and External Training

DSS also adopted a risk-based approach to providing cleared defense contractors with tailored counterintelligence services supported by a realistic assessment of threats to classified information and technology resident at each facility. To close the functional gaps that exist, DSS will continue to integrate field Counterintelligence Specialists, Industrial Security Representatives and Information System Security Personnel to proactively mitigate against espionage and collection attempts by foreign intelligence and security service threats.

DSS is developing CI Training Requirements and Competencies to assist in the identification of job qualifications, core competencies and training requirements specific to DSS personnel. By educating Industrial Security Representatives and Information System Security Personnel on basic CI competencies and skills, DSS will enhance the "every person is a sensor" concept and serve as a tremendous force multiplier in the field for DSS.

Prioritizing Suspicious Contact Reports

Contractors cleared under the NISP have an obligation to identify and report suspicious contacts and potential collection attempts to DSS, as outlined in the National Industrial Security Program Operating Manual (NISPOM). DSS prioritizes the Suspicious Contact Reports (SCRs) received from cleared industry into four categories, with the most serious being Category I (Targeting Confirmed) and Category II (Targeting Probable). Category I & II SCRs are promptly reported to DSS's Field Counterintelligence Specialists so the information can be quickly shared with the larger DoD CI and Law Enforcement communities. This prioritization effort means critical information is getting to DSS field personnel and industry more quickly to identify and counter CI threats.

Publication of the trend analysis report

DSS publishes a report detailing suspicious contacts occurring within the cleared defense contractor community. This reports is based on an analysis of Suspicious Contact Reports (SCRs) from cleared industry that DSS considers indicative of efforts by entities to target defense-related personnel, and information and technologies developed or maintained by the Cleared Defense Community. This year, DSS published both a classified and an unclassified version of the "2008 Targeting U.S. Technologies: A Trend Analysis of Reporting from Defense Industry." Since the number and danger posed by cyber threats continues to increase, the 2008 Trends included a special section about the use of cyber space as a collection medium.

> **ANOTHER UNDERLYING THEME IN THE BUDGET RECOMMENDATIONS IS THE NEED TO THINK ABOUT FUTURE CONFLICTS IN A DIFFERENT WAY. TO RECOGNIZE THAT THE BLACK AND WHITE DISTINCTION BETWEEN CONVENTIONAL WAR AND IRREGULAR WAR IS AN OUTDATED MODEL. IN REALITY, THE FUTURE IS AND WILL BE MORE COMPLEX. WHERE ALL CONFLICT WILL RANGE ALONG A BROAD SPECTRUM OF OPERATIONS AND LETHALITY. WHERE EVEN NEAR-PEER COMPETITORS WILL USE IRREGULAR OR ASYMMETRIC TACTICS AND NON-STATE ACTORS MAY HAVE WEAPONS OF MASS DESTRUCTION OR SOPHISTICATED MISSILES.**
>
> **SECRETARY OF DEFENSE ROBERT M. GATES**

Office of the Designated Approving Authority
Accreditation of information systems

The Office of the Designated Approving Authority (ODAA) is the government entity responsible for approving and accrediting cleared contractor information systems (IS) to process classified data nationwide. As a part of the accreditation process, the ODAA ensures IS security controls are in place to limit the risk of compromising national security information. In particular, the ODAA is strengthening cleared defense industry managed IT systems and has promulgated system security controls and user access controls to mitigate cyber threats and protect classified information. DSS is working with industry to implement these procedures which will help DSS better protect against threats to classified IT systems in industry.

DSS is also developing a cyber security strategy designed to make classified IT Systems in Industry impenetrable. We anticipate the strategy will include education and training, enhanced policy and procedures, enhanced information sharing, cooperative intelligence analysis, collective use of expertise, and collaboration.

DSS published Industrial Security Letter 2009-01 to clarify the safeguarding standards used in determining if an Information System in industry is eligible for accreditation. Two documents — "Manual for the Certification and Accreditation of Classified Systems under the National Industrial Security Program Operating Manual (NISPOM)" and, "Standardization of Baseline Technical Security Configurations" contain a set of safeguards that DSS will apply when making an accreditation decision. The ISL highlights and outlines the expectations set by these standards. The safeguards outlined in both the ODAA Manual and Baseline Standards will not apply to every information system and after a full review, DSS will consider deviations from the standards on a case-by-case basis. Both the Manual and the Baseline Standards will be updated and published by DSS as necessary.

Foreign Ownership, Control or Influence
Streamlining the Process

Foreign investment plays an important role in maintaining the vitality of the U.S. industrial base. While it is the policy of the U.S. Government to allow foreign investment consistent with the national security interests of the United States, foreign investment in U.S. defense industry poses a unique risk to the protection of classified information. A company is considered to be operating under FOCI whenever a foreign interest has the power, direct or indirect, whether or not exercised, and whether or not exercisable, to direct or decide matters affecting the management or operations of that company in a manner which may result in unauthorized access to classified information or may adversely affect the performance of classified contracts. DSS adjudicates FOCI factors of cleared contractors participating in the National Industrial Security Program (NISP) on behalf of DoD and 23 non-DoD government agencies.

DSS greatly improved its handling of FOCI cases resulting in a more operationally agile process. DSS field employees are empowered to adjudicate cases requiring minor FOCI mitigation arrangements. The result is a more efficient and expedient process. DSS has also integrated field personnel into complex FOCI cases to ensure that the proposed mitigation mechanisms are reasonable and inspectable.

The Office of the Designated Approving Authority (ODAA) developed a process to assist in FOCI reviews that will assess the electronic communication plan and information system infrastructure for those companies that fall under FOCI. The process was developed to mirror and leverage as much as possible the certification and accreditation process performed for the Defense Industrial Base. This new process provides a formal, documented process to evaluate the IT posture of companies under FOCI.

> **WE WILL SAFEGUARD WHAT WE MUST TO PROTECT THE AMERICAN PEOPLE, BUT WE WILL ALSO ENSURE THE ACCOUNTABILITY AND OVERSIGHT THAT IS THE HALLMARK OF OUR CONSTITUTIONAL SYSTEM.**
>
> **PRESIDENT BARACK OBAMA**

DSS stood up an Analytic Branch to analyze and apply all available information to the mitigation strategies for companies under FOCI. The branch collects data on individual companies to create effective, specific mitigation strategies for companies under FOCI. The branch also monitors trends to provide a strategic analysis of the types of foreign investment vehicles and the U.S. companies or technologies sought by foreign investors.

Of particular concern to DSS and the Department are the impact of sovereign wealth funds (SWF), hedge funds, and other financial arrangements. These financial tools can combine to provide capital to acquire and manage large corporations, while the ultimate source of the capital is difficult to trace. DSS must better understand their impacts and make adjustments in security organization, doctrine, training and personnel. Emerging financial arrangements like these highlight the increasingly complex burden of determining the appropriate foreign investment countermeasures in support of national security.

> **CYBERSPACE HAS BECOME A KEY DOMAIN - IN A SIMILAR CONTEXT TO LAND, AIR, AND SEA - THROUGH WHICH GOVERNMENT AND MILITARY LEADERS CAN PURSUE, ACHIEVE, AND ENHANCE THEIR OBJECTIVES... AND, THIS HAS CHANGED AT A PACE FEW WOULD HAVE ANTICIPATED.**
>
> **SECRETARY OF DEFENSE ROBERT M. GATES**

Training
Reaccreditation

Accreditation is a status granted to an educational institution or program that assures quality and assists in the improvement of the institute or program. The standards for national accreditation are set by the Council on Occupational Education (COE) and are outlined in the council's Handbook of Accreditation. The DSS Academy was reaccredited for six years by the COE in February.

A team from the COE visited the Academy to review the Academy's accreditation self-study exhibits, and then interviewed SETA/DSS Academy staff and students to ensure compliance. The COE Team determined that the DSS Academy is in full compliance with all eleven standards of accreditation and the conditions of accreditation.

More courses

The demand for professional security training continues to grow. To meet this demand, the DSS Academy expanded its course offerings, seeking news ways to provide training and creating tools to support security education. SETA is moving from classroom-based training to more web-based training, which allows DSS to deliver training to those who need it, when they need it. During the last year, 10 new courses were offered by SETA, including:

- Security Classification Guidance
- Original Classification
- Derivative Classification
- Business Structures in the NISP
- Industrial Security Facilities Database for DSS Users
- Physical Security Measures Course
- Getting Started Seminar for New Facility Security Officers (FSO)

The courses were developed in response to identified requirements. For instance, a course could be in response to a regulatory/policy mandate, a DoD stakeholder (Military Service Component, Defense Agency or DoD Industrial Contractor Community) articulated a formal request, or as a request for an intervention needed for security professionals/practitioners to meet a competency level associated with a DoD Community approved skill standard in one of the security disciplines (i.e., physical, personal, industrial, or information security).

The DSS Academy schedules regular and recurring security curriculum planning and review meetings to directly engage security community representatives in the testing and evaluation of courseware and content prior to deployment.

SETA established a certification program for the DoD security adjudicator community and the Special Access Program (SAP) community. SETA is working on a similar program for DoD Security Professionals, as well as certifications for DSS Security Professionals.

> **... WE CANNOT ACHIEVE RESILIENCE OR REACH OUR FULL POTENTIAL WITHOUT SECURITY. THIS IS TREMENDOUSLY IMPORTANT GIVEN THE KIND OF THREATS THE NORTH AMERICAN CONTINENT FACES AT THE DAWN OF THE 21ST CENTURY.**
>
> **SECDEF ROBERT M. GATES**

More job aids

In addition to formal courses, the Academy expanded its training products and services, providing eight new security information/job aid videos, with 11 more in development. Two new videos offered by SETA include a new security awareness training video, "Need-To-Know," which provides a short video vignette regarding the fundamental need-to-know security principle, and a video describing the transformation of the Facility Security Officer (FSO) curriculum into a distance learning format.

> **" I BELIEVE THAT WE CANNOT SOLVE THE CHALLENGES OF OUR TIME UNLESS WE SOLVE THEM TOGETHER. WE WILL NOT BE SAFE IF WE SEE NATIONAL SECURITY AS A WEDGE THAT DIVIDES AMERICA — IT CAN AND MUST BE A CAUSE THAT UNITES US AS ONE PEOPLE AND AS ONE NATION. WE'VE DONE SO BEFORE IN TIMES THAT WERE MORE PERILOUS THAN OURS. WE WILL DO SO ONCE AGAIN. "**
>
> **PRESIDENT BARACK OBAMA**

Improvements in PSI-I processing
Personnel Security Investigations for Industry (PSI-I) Requirements Survey

In April 2008, DSS deployed its annual web-based survey to 10,953 cleared Industry Facility Security Officers representing 12,189 cleared facilities for the purposes of projecting PSI-I requirements. The projections are the key component in Future Years Defense Program (FYDP) DSS/DoD program planning and budgeting for NISP security clearances. With more than 83 percent of cleared contractor facilities responding, representing 92 percent of the cleared contractor population, the survey is a highly effective tool in projecting contractor security clearance requirements. Projections provided from the survey in FY07 were 103.9 percent of actual submissions. At the close of FY08, industry clearance eligibility submissions were .9 percent above projections, which is well within the Office of Management and Budget mandate that the survey results be +/- 5 percent of actual submissions.

Reducing the PSI-I backlog

The Defense Industrial Security Clearance Office adjudicates PSI-Is on behalf of DoD and 23 other Federal agencies in the National Industrial Security Program. During FY08, the pending case inventory at DISCO declined from 34,630 to 3,394, marking a 90 percent reduction in pending adjudication inventory.

FY08 DISCO PENDING ADJUDICATIONS CHART

Case Type	Oct-07 (Start of Q1)	Mar-08 (End of Q2)	Jun-08 (End of Q3)	Sep-08 (End of Q4)	Delta (Q1 vs Q4)
NACLC	11,449	488	240	1,953	-83%
SSBI	9,337	5,625	30	354	-96%
SBPR	4,899	3,752	5,973	757	-85%
PPR	8,945	4,923	4,210	330	-96%
Total Pending	34,630	14,788	10,453	3,394	-90%

IRTPA Guidelines

The Intelligence Reform and Terrorism Prevention Act of 2004 (IRTPA) mandated specific goals for improving timeliness of both personnel security investigations and adjudications. DISCO exceeded the mandated IRTPA guidelines for completion of adjudications. DISCO also achieved significant success in reducing average adjudication process times as well as increasing the number of adjudications completed.

- In FY08, DISCO completed 90% of initial adjudications in 20 days. This exceeded the 25-day intermediate IRTPA goal established by the Office of Management and Budget by five days.

- DISCO increased the number of initial personnel security clearance adjudications measured by IRTPA by 35% from FY07 to FY08 (from 111,415 in FY07 to 150,333 in FY08).

- DISCO increased the number of all adjudications (initial and other) by 38%, from 139,345 in FY07 to 191,914 in FY08.

- DISCO increased the number of interim personnel security clearance eligibilities granted by 11%, from 82,550 in FY07 to 92,350 in FY08.

- DISCO increased the number of personnel security clearance eligibilities granted by 30%, from 139,407 in FY07 to 181,179 in FY08.

Automation initiatives
Automated fingerprint submission

All initial national security investigations require the submission of fingerprints as part of the request for investigation to the Office of Personnel Management. Secure Web Fingerprint Transmission (SWFT) is a program that permits electronic submission of fingerprints for Personnel Security Investigations for Industry. SWFT can capture fingerprint images, upload the images to the DSS server, temporarily store these electronic files on the server, and then release the file to OPM. In July 2008, DSS launched a pilot with a test group of industry partners, who provided the first electronic fingerprint files via the DSS secure web connection to the DSS system. DSS forwarded these files to OPM's fingerprint system, completing the end-to-end system connection. The pilot proved successful and the system is expected to be fielded in July 2009. The system can store in excess of 15,000 fingerprint submissions, notify industry users of the transmission status, and provide account management and metrics collection features. When fully deployed, the system will reduce fingerprint rejection rates as well as improve investigative timeliness. Industry is supplying the equipment to capture the electronic fingerprints.

> FUTURE ADVERSARIES WILL CONTINUE TO EMPLOY NEW READILY AVAILABLE TECHNOLOGIES IN SINISTER WAYS. THEY WILL ADAPT AND DEVELOP NEW TACTICS, TECHNIQUES, AND PROCEDURES AS FAST AS THEY CAN IMAGINE WAYS TO GAIN ANY ADVANTAGE OVER US, TO BETTER UNDERSTAND OUR DECISION CYCLE. THIS KIND OF WARFARE WILL REQUIRE INNOVATIVE, VERSATILE LEADERS AND CAPABILITIES WITH THE MAXIMUM POSSIBLE FLEXIBILITY AND AGILITY TO DEAL WITH THE WIDEST POSSIBLE RANGE OF CONFLICT.
>
> SECRETARY OF DEFENSE ROBERT M. GATES

The following case studies provide lessons learned for DSS,
the cleared defense community and Government Contracting Activities.

Accreditation of Missile Defense Agency (MDA) Wide Body Airborne Platform (WASP)

LESSON LEARNED:
Whether government contracting authority, program manager or cleared defense industry, think of DSS early in the process. DSS personnel are flexible and will work to ensure the mission is not affected. DSS can ensure delivery of the best product possible when given adequate time to address an issue.

In November 2008, Missile Defense Agency (MDA) program personnel contacted the DSS Southern Region Designated Approving Authority (RDAA) concerning plans for accreditation of a wide body airborne platform (WASP) information system. This system supported an MDA mission critical test that was scheduled for December 5 on the west coast and MDA was relying on the WASP system to collect data for analysis of the planned test.

The contractor involved did not properly plan for accreditation and had not developed a system security plan (SSP) for DSS to review. MDA requested DSS assistance so they could proceed with the test.

ODAA personnel assisted the contractor in preparing the SSP. This entailed significant coordination between ODAA and the contractor, including an explanation of the requirements and guidance/support for reviews and corrections prior to a final submission. DSS issued an Interim Approval to Operate on Dec. 1, 2008, allowing MDA to proceed with their test

FOCI Case Study

LESSON LEARNED:
DSS has the flexibility and tools to mitigate the foreign influence on most any business structure. Again, involve DSS early in the process to ensure valuable time and resources are not wasted.

Last fall, a large cleared U.S. company went through the Committee on Foreign Investment in the United States (CFIUS) process as part of being acquired by a foreign company. The foreign company is effectively controlled by its foreign government based on foreign government stock ownership and voting rights. The U.S. company has a large number of proscribed contracts (Top Secret, COMSEC, RD, SAP, or SCI) with multiple government customers.

Under 10 USC 2536, DoD is prohibited from issuing contracts requiring access to proscribed information to companies under foreign government control unless the Secretary of Defense grants a waiver.

DSS is implementing special field inspection teams to ensure consistency of enforcement across all the company's cleared facilities.

Company A notified DSS, that a former employee had mishandled classified information on their unclassified network. During the course of the administrative inquiry, the company discovered:

- Hidden and encrypted files under the employee's last name
- More than 800 folders containing more than 10,000 files
- The folders were hidden from view and permissions denied to Network Administrators as well as anyone else
- These permissions had to be set manually and deliberately
- No incident report was made in JPAS

The Administrative Inquiry revealed a previous security violation by the employee who had created a classified document on a Company laptop. Again, no incident report was made in JPAS.

A second company notified DSS of a suspicious contact report that detailed an employee who was observed "placing things in a backpack," in an area where this behavior appeared out of the norm. This occurred two weeks after the original notification and as it turned out, both reports were on the same individual.

The appropriate government agency was notified and an investigation initiated. During the initial phases of the investigation, it was discovered that this same individual allegedly stole proprietary information from a third company. This third company did not pursue the information for fear of "bad" or "negative press" since the employee had departed the company.

Search warrants were issued for the individual's home, car, and work space. Thousands of documents, computer media, etc, at all three locations were discovered; much of it classified (Top Secret, Secret, and Confidential). It may take up to one year to go through all of the confiscated media to determine the number of charges that should be levied.

This case shows several good things:

- Hidden files were discovered at the first company
- Once discovered, the hard drive was handled in accordance with the highest level of classification pending DSS retrieval and/or disposal directions
- The Facility Security Officer did a great job alerting the right folks and working closely with DSS

And many not so good things:

- The first company had no mechanisms in place to prevent this individual from hiding several thousands files and encrypting them on their unclassified LAN
- The company did not follow-up when the employee turned in a laptop after "wiping" the hard drive – an unauthorized practice
- The companies chose not to report or utilize JPAS concerning the initial security violations committed by the employee, because the employee no longer worked for them
- DSS did not follow-up on the hard-drive retrieval in a timely manner
- DSS did not initially pursue because there was no apparent foreign nexus. It was deemed a security violation.

LESSON LEARNED:
DSS reviewed the shortfalls in this case and is implementing a proposed mechanism for capturing, reporting and in the near future linking information from violations / administrative inquiries more quickly.

DSS PRIORITIES & PREPARING FOR THE FUTURE

For the coming year, DSS will continue to enhance and expand the National Industrial Security Program and reinvigorate the Security Education Training and Awareness Program. Our priorities are:

Counterintelligence

DSS will aggressively focus on cyber threats — an increasing threat and complex challenge. DSS will continue to expand its CI staff to better assist customers in mitigating espionage and collection attempts by foreign intelligence and security services, to include exploitation of cyber space and the threat posed by insiders.

FOCI

DSS will continue to improve on the FOCI process. DSS commissioned an outside study of the FOCI process to look for improvements and once identified, proposed improvements will be implemented as soon as possible.

Training

The DSS Academy is constantly searching out innovative methods to deliver training and increasing the scope of the training offered. Currently, there are more than 25 courses in development, which includes building a curriculum for certification of the DSS work force.

Preparing for the future

While proud of our successes, DSS continuously seeks to improve our performance as the premier provider of personnel and industrial security services in the Department of Defense (DoD). Through new ideas, innovations and expanded technology, DSS will continue to ensure the security of our nation and our warfighters.